IT STARTS WITH THE END

IT STARTS WITH THE END

Lauren Rose Lenyi

RESOURCE *Publications* • Eugene, Oregon

IT STARTS WITH THE END

Resource Publications
An Imprint of Wipf and Stock Publishers
199 W. 8th Ave., Suite 3
Eugene, OR 97401

www.wipfandstock.com

PAPERBACK ISBN: 978-1-6667-5197-0
HARDCOVER ISBN: 978-1-6667-5198-7
EBOOK ISBN: 978-1-6667-5199-4

AUGUST 25, 2022 11:09 AM

To Grandma,
Without you, I would not have the courage to write.

Contents

Trigger Warning

Sexual Assault and Trauma
Emotional Trauma
Sexism
Depression
Anxiety

Dear Reader,

Firstly, I want to thank you for deciding to read my book. Though the contents within are about my life and ordeal with sexual assault, I know that far too many of you may share some of my feelings and experiences too. I hope this book can bring you the same solace I received while writing *It Starts with the End*. Remember you are stronger than you know.

Love,
Lauren Lenyi

THE END

I hate the fact that you broke me,
More times than I care to admit.

I will never forget
All the times that we spoke.
Whenever you overtook the conversation,
In those moments the world shook.

I should have known,
How could I be so blind?
A friend I called you,
Oh, those were the times.

I thought I deserved to be punished,
For my actions, my choices.
I was merely a child,
When you stole my smile.

Your name won't leave my lips.
The way you walk, the way you talk
Seals those fatal words in.

I never let myself feel,
The weight of it all
Till it was too heavy
I couldn't help but fall.
But did my legs buckle from the weight,
Or were they kicked out from under me
By a familiar face?
No one could relate,
To my all-consuming feelings of hate.
The hate I have for you, for me,
For the world that cradles this agony.

Was I the one who created this mess?
Or was I merely supplied a Band-Aid
To heal and rest.
But I had a wound
Much more demanding than that.
The scar is still there, nasty and loud.
One day I hope
It will disappear.
Out of sight, but not out of mind.
No doubt I will remember
For the rest of my life.

they
won't
understand you here.
they don't understand your tears
when the drops become puddles
a face is reflected here. you don't recognize
that it is yours. the water rises, the
smell of salt overbearing. the tears
at your neck choke you like a collar.
the thought occurs,

if
you stop
crying the inevitable
won't happen. but how can you stop?
do you want to stop? and once you're
submerged in water they surely would notice,
but will they understand? that
the tears that drown you were
brought on by them.

I can't go back,
Not even if I wanted to.
The past haunts my present,
I'm sure it will haunt my future too.
As long as you're there
The trauma continues
To beat me,
Break me,
Remind me of you.
Of a time in which I wasn't me
Because of you.

I will never get closure
From going back.
This was not a place of peace,
Remember all I've said.

You will see your friends,
Your mentors for years,

But what about those
I can't stand to be near?
The ones who did nothing,
Didn't offer a dime,
Who couldn't bother to help
And save a life on their time.

So, keep your opinions to yourself.
I've heard it all before.
Your magic solutions won't work
On a girl that's been cursed.
I don't care what you say,
I care what you don't.
It's quite simple, you see,
If you did you would have shut your mouth,
And stopped talking by now,
About things, you could care less
To hear about.

Now tell me
As you read this,
Did you find your closure?
Are you fulfilled and content?
I think I know the answer.
Do you?
I hope you got your closure.

I've roamed these halls,
Barren of people
But not the memories.
The touches,
Pain,
And numbness.
My skin crawls,
And my heart aches,
For the time in which
I didn't hate this place.
It's true.
God, it's true.
I hate this part of my life,
And I fucking hate you.
I wish I could go back
And fix the mistakes,
I wasn't allowed to make it.

There were moments and memories
Where we were blissfully content.
When we smiled and laughed together,
Amidst the glorious spring breeze,
Underneath canopied trees.
Everything was cordial,
Consensual,
Until it was not.
How am I supposed to process
That.
It went from slaps on the back,
To fondling my breasts.
Gawking at me
Without a shred of dignity.
Texting me the most heinous things.
Following me down the halls,
You were far too tall
I couldn't disappear,
Into my crowd of peers.
You were faster, stronger,
And more masculine than me.
Who was I to think anyone would believe me?
That I held any kind of power
After what you did to me.
Yet, I'm still here.
Grasping at the breezy memories,
Of kindness and friendship,
That linger within me.
For better or for worse?
A blessing or a curse?
I'm not so sure.

They turn a blind eye
To The Bodies' cuts, bruises, and scars.
Their consciousness is focused,
And hearts attached too,
To the ones who stole
The Body's virtue.
As if they deserve
The empathy they lack.
As if their pity
Is as justifiable as their negligence.
Remorse, sweet friend,
You've left us again.

They say they care
But their eyes scream otherwise.
Their insincerity reveals,
That they want a break
From the inconvenience,
Of The Bodies existence.
Of alleged experiences,
Of the pain
They now must experience.

Yet, The Bodies are the only ones who suffer here,
As they have suffered before,
As they will suffer after.
The Bodies, who are damned to speak
And never be heard.
The Bodies who listen
And hear all spoken and unspoken words.
The Bodies who are cursed to watch everything,
All, except what they so desperately need to see.

The Bodies with no names, no personalities.
No smiles, no laughter.
No hearts, no souls.
No help, no hope.

No. Time.

No . . .

There is not enough time
In this doomed universe.
Because time has already taken its toll . . .

And the Bodies are forced to decompose.

I hate my words,
My writing, my thoughts.
Because they mean
That I still care.
That I can't control
This black hole of despair.

I'm in the trenches
Going to war,
Each time the pen hits the paper.
While you're enjoying the high life,
Living without a care for life.

I've done this over and over again.
Sat here writing, till the bitter end,
But nothing changes.
I empty my head,
The pain trudges on,
And you remain
Oblivious, in oblivion.
Not knowing there was even a beginning,
Let alone an end.

And even if you saw my words,
Read them aloud or in your head,
I guarantee,
My sweet misery,
Oh, you wouldn't believe
You could do such a thing.

All I'm asking for
Is to not be made uncomfortable,
In my own flesh.
To be me in public without fear.
To not have my palms sweat when a man walks nearby.
For my heart to be calm when he brushes my shoulder.
To be at ease in a place where I should always feel safe.

I dress up, I'm a slut.
I open my mouth, I'm a bitch.
I flirt, and I'm begging to be hurt.

All I ask is
To not be sexually assaulted.
To not be harassed,
Catcalled,
Or stalked.
Why must these requests cause unfathomable distress?
Can sympathy be real, or pity desist?
Am I allowed to exist?

I am not even demanding these basic human rights.
I am just asking politely,
To be given an inch
When I should be kicking and screaming,
Fighting for all I've missed,
Fighting for all who have been dismissed.

As I know the question will arise,
I did speak up to tell my side.
Though whether or not I did,
Is a moot point,
I still want you to know
That I told people in power
In an effort to gain hope.

When I spoke the first time,
Emotions ran high.
It was after a mandatory high school
Training exercise.
I pulled them aside, cried,
And died a little inside.
After the conversation, I felt seen.
I really believed they would do something.

Of course, it was to the detriment of my safety.
I wanted to be anonymous,
They put a target on my back,
And He tried to contact me.
I ignored the texts,
The calls,
Yet he continued to search for me.
He cornered me in the hall,
Demanded I tell him what I had said,
I found it odd he did not ask *why?* instead.
I told him to fuck off.
I ran back to the people with power.
I spoke again.

They said he had guessed that it was me,
When I knew for a fact,

There were more women.
It was never just me.
When I pleaded with shaky hands and
A heavy heart,
All they did was stare down at me,
In my outfit I wore to avoid the heat.

Great, gawk at me.
Just like the boy,
Whom you promised to keep away from me.

They told me not to worry,
They would handle it.
I never heard anything from them again.
I guess their power only stretched,
To those, they thought deserved respect.
I was left alone, scared, and vulnerable
For another year and a half.
Knowing he was doing worse things to others,
Not knowing if he would hurt me again.
Believing I was overreacting,
Or that it was all in my head.

But I want you to know,
That I spoke up.
stood tall,
I did what I thought was best.
And got pushed down yet again
By a boy.
And a boy's best friend:
Power, with no end.

Have you decided who you're truly meant to be?
How did you do it?
If you know the answer, please tell me.
Bestow to me this knowledge,
So, you could free me.
Be selfless please and fucking free me too.
Would you?

Where do I begin,
When I want to divulge my sins?
I don't know if this feeling is real.
Did I love you then?
Did I become infatuated
With the idea of friendship instead?
You never failed to disappoint.
And I came back,
When I was given the chance.
But was it a choice?
When you are ensnared,
By a magnetic force,
Without being aware that it's there.

I was not told
That the person on the other end,
Would make me writhe in pain
To the end.
I saw the end coming, though,
The sorrow therein.
And I stayed for my fate.
For the one I loved or at least adored.
The intimacy we shared,
As friends not foes
Which would lead to nothing more,
Than Anger.
Deceit.
Treachery.
And a toxic bond that lasts till this day,
Which I can't quite be sure is real or fake.
That is my sin.
For which I must bear
Forevermore,
This I know for sure.

You're out of my life,
Yet not out of my head.
Your grasp on me has not faltered,
Only tightened instead.
The distance is futile,
Obsolete,
I'm incomplete,
Or so I've been made to believe.
The closure I hoped for
Will never be.
I look longingly at the future,
At the plans I have made.
The past
I wished to forsake,
I cannot shake.
I don't think I'll ever be free,
From the unsettling nightmares,
From fear, I get in the streets.
And you're the one to blame,
I think?

Why must my brain try to justify
The damage you have done to me.
I have dreams where I am the antagonist,
And you the protagonist.
I don't want it to be true,
Yet more often than not,
I believe it, I do.

And when I wake,
Chaos is still in its rightful place.
Did I see your car?
That shade of blue taunts me.
Did you walk past my place?
You only live a block away.

Am I going insane?
There are billions of people on Earth
But I only see you.
I know you see me too.
And when I do,
You look filled with shame,
Guilt-ridden on your face.
But unlike me, it does not affect you.
At least, not at the same magnitude.
I don't think I will ever understand that look.
It's there whenever you see me,
what does it mean?
So much emotion,
All selfish, maybe?

Must you invade my thoughts,
My dreams?
Every man I see
Is you smiling down at me.
I wish it wasn't me.
I wish it wasn't you.
Please stay the fuck away from me,
So I won't come crawling back to you.
I beg you, please,
Don't summon your power over me.
Say your goodbyes,
Stop making me cry.
It's happened before, it will happen again.
I wish it weren't true,
But if you walk back now,
I'll walk back too.
And meet you halfway,
Where we will stay
And I
Will kneel
For you.

Why doesn't my brain
Give a shit about me?
Why doesn't it stop
These swarming thoughts
The ones that make me
Turn and toss
Until those morning rays
Burn those thoughts away
But don't breathe yet
Because I will soon regress
Back to that time
That place
That wasteful state
In which
All I can do
Is sit in shame,
Blame,
And continue
With this miserable game
One which my brain
All but creates
The game progresses
And I do too
Without a brain
That gives a shit
About What
I
Want
To
Do.

As I stare at this blank page
Pondering how to fill it,
Tears line my eyes.
Because I know that it will be
The same thing once more.

The page will be stained
A dreary black,
With words, I don't want to write,
Because they are all about you.
How even now,
I can feel your hands around my neck.
Your bitter breath in my ear.
As you release a stupid laugh,
Or haughty quips.

I see your slanted gate as you walk away,
And back again to me.
Every time.
I sit to write
To pass the time, to fulfill my passion.
The words I will not speak,
Are released and transformed
To an unbearable scratch.
A scar on every piece of work.
As if your hands have traveled
Away from my neck,
And into my hands,
Using me to write
To preserve yourself herein.

When my tears spill over,
They are not for you,

But for me.
As I hope they will flush away,
The words, the ink,
The ghost of you.
I pray this cleansing will come true.

I'm going to visit the sea,
And let it drown me.
I'll let the saltwater soak my skin,
And the tide pull my
Innocence,
Trust,
And hope in.
The fish can nip at my heels.
The jellyfish can cuddle me close.
The Sun can char my skin.
The seaweed can strangle me.
The riptide can pull me under.
Water can fill my lungs
And I'll close my eyes,
Purse my lips,
And simply allow it all in.
It does not make a difference,
Does it?

How am I to be fulfilled,
When all I can think about is what haunts me still?
I long for smiles,
To cry tears of joy.
My heart is so desperately wishing for it all to end,
How long will it take to heal, to mend?
I thought I had a little
But I still feel stuck in the middle
Of a world that's moving around me,
As I stay frozen, day and night.

When will there be a day,
Where I don't think of those boys?
When they will stop stripping me bare,
Of my future,
My hopes,
My humanity,
My clothes.
And just leave well enough alone.
How much longer,
Can I continue with your
hands around my breasts?
I don't want to live like this,
I am so very sick.

What will happen when you bury me?
By the time I die, what will be my legacy?
Will they honor and cherish me?
Will there even be a *They* to remember me?

I wonder if they will bury me near my family,
Under a willow tree, or give me to the fates that be?
Will the tears come quickly with heartfelt compliments?
Or have the tears turned to mist?
Compassion be damned, will I be missed?

Are they going to follow my will?
Let the dead woman pick?
Perhaps they will scatter me, is that what I wish?
If I am to be buried,
My accolades will profess my distress.
With a brief eulogy mentioning
The little good deeds, I've achieved.
Solemn words by the few people
who can be seen.
Disgrace embroidered on their face,
As they lay me down to rest.
And bury me and my memory.

I wish I could say that will never be.
But I know all too well
What may become of me.
So, I understand if there is no grave,
No ashes that remain,
Or even a *They* to recall my name.
I will gladly be forgotten
If it allows me time and space,
To rest, at peace,

In the knowledge that as it were
I once was me.

My Glass Box is not my home.
I was put here unwillingly.
I don't know how I got here.
I was asleep
Dreaming in bed,
When I awoke in a prison,
My prism.
Cold, crystal-clear glass.
Alone and vulnerable.
Welcomed only by an eerie silence.

People would come,
To stare at me.
Laugh,
Joke,
Forget,
Repeat.
Yet they can't see me,
Not really.
In the beginning, I would talk to them,
Screaming obscenities and pleas,
Yelling until my voice was raw.
I'd sob until I went as blind as the passersby.
I'd punch the glass
Shatter my knuckles,
As I hoped to shatter the glass.
But I made no mark.
To my Glass Box,
Or them.

Some days I will stare at them,
Searching for an ounce of compassion in their eyes,
A glimpse of humanity.
I wonder if any of them put me here?
Do they know who did?

There is no point in dwelling
On why they do nothing.
My Glass Box is not for me,
It's for them.
I'm just an attraction to consume,
A means to an end.

Everything disappears in my Glass Box,
My tears,
My voice,
My soul.
Yet, the world around me never changes.
My Glass Box is
Simple,
Sterile.
Enormous,
Empty.
Prison,
Perfect.
Heaven,
Hell.
Limbo.
A fucking Glass Box.

Who gave you the fucking right,
To waltz in and ruin my life?
To take what was mine.

You have caused me so much pain,
You will never understand,
The damage you have done,
The trauma you created.
Going outside makes me die inside.
Panic attacks were a part of my daily routine.
I could not be held
By my friends and family,
Because the parts of my body you touched,
Are still in shock.

I hated what I could not change,
My curves,
My lips,
My hips.
You are a stain on this Earth.
Your legacy is destruction.
I hate you
You had no fucking right,
To cause me to lose,
Years of my life.

How am I supposed to be okay,
When my days are filled with
Noon Nightmares?

How am I supposed to be okay,
When everyone around me
Is so much more than okay?

How am I supposed to be okay,
When my mind is gray
And the fog won't go away?

How am I supposed to be okay,
When everyone remains ignorant
Of my pain?

How am I supposed to be okay,
When the bad days are everyday?

How am I supposed to be okay,
When society's morals are fading away?
How am I supposed to be okay,

When people are telling
And not showing me the way?

How am I supposed to be okay,
When I have never been that way.

All you left me with was pain.
You pushed me down the rabbit hole,
And I screamed out all the way.
No one offered to help the voice that cried out in vain.

I landed with a thud,
A thundering crack to my head.
Blood seeped on the tiles,
Black and white stained a cursed red.

No rhymes, riddles, or shanties were sung to me,
No bunnies or flowers came to comfort me.
Tweddle Dee and Tweddle Dumb
Resided up above.
There was not a soul to seek security from.

I waited for a ray of sunshine to warm me up
But I knew all too well,
The Sun would not come up.

I waited for the White Rabbit to save me,
To say,

Come with me.
Oh, Alice, oh, Alice, where have you been?

But all I found were Demons,
Cackling at my misery,
My gullibility.

Still, I hid and hoped.
For years, for centuries,

Till I could not sit still anymore.
I was already down the Rabbit Hole,
How much farther could I go?

I walked into the darkness,
To the Demons therein.
Their laughter died on their tongues,
As they welcomed me in.
Down in the deep, deep, dark,
A new place to begin.

I stayed there, sipping tea with my Demons,
Going mad, mad, mad.

Oh, Alice, where have you been?
Oh, Alice, oh, Alice, where will you go?
Now that you've fallen down, down the rabbit hole?

But I am no longer easygoing Alice,
Longing for the tulips to grace me with their song

Woe is me; Woe is me.

Their pity only taunts me.

I suppose being pushed down a hole,
Does not affect the White Rabbit
Oh, no,
He would not help me now,
He will not help me ever.
And even if he offered,
I'd refuse downright.
Because I will not use his perfect white paw to rise.

My Demons cracked me open,
And cleaned me up, too.
The darkness embraced me once more,
Before I made my way back to that dreadful rabbit hole.

I gripped the sides of the hideous hole,
And climbed up, up, up,
Wondering how high it would go.
Would I fall again, or climb back up and continue to pretend?

My fingernails broke,
My will broke,
But when did that happen?
When I fell or when I rose?

Am I mad or am I sane?
Either way, what do I do with the pain?
Will my indifference make it go away?
And which is worse: the former or the latter?
Tell me Mad Hatter, tell me it's the latter.

I reached the top of the hole,
To a World, I wish I didn't know,
The ghastly light, all I've ever known.
I wanted it would go away,
For I want the twilight, not the dawn,
To stay by my side from now on.

I collapsed at the end.

I saw you straight ahead,
Not a care in the world,
Not a thought in your head.
But this is my dream after all.
I'll decide where it'll go, how it will end,
This would be the last time I'd have to pretend.

I sang sweet nothings
And laughed softly,
But not at your jokes.
It was only to gain your trust
And provide me hope.

I led you to the hollow ground,
As the dusk set in.
No fear in sight, how lucky you've been.

Oh, Alice,
It's almost your time to play, my dear.
Oh, Alice, oh, Alice,
Let the madness control you from here.

So, I did.
And that's when I pushed you in,
All alone,

Down . . .

Down . . .

Down the rabbit hole.

THE BEGINNING

I once believed that you controlled my mind.
A puppet with unbreakable string,
Weaved through my weary skin.
Now I realize the truth
And though it's been right in front of me
All along,
It's rather easy to miss.
It was me and not you
Who held the pen.
And in my weakest moments,
I lost my grip.
The ink slipped and stained my wrists.
The paper smeared with self-pity.
I'm trying to move on from this.
I find it just as hard to say,
As it is to do.
But I can push forward,
Let the ink dry,
And burn the pages
With you still trapped inside.

The journey to heal,
Has been a somber path,
A non-linear trail
Obscured,
Perturbed,
And yet I endured.
Through all the trials and tribulations,
The tears and heartache,
The path smoothes over,
The fog clears,
And the tears that once flowed
Create flowers that bloom all year.

I bought into the lies,
The stereotypes,
The ideas pumped into
The veins of humanity
By a masculine entity,
Fools in positions of power.
But it's time to usurp them,
And relearn the truth:
You can go back.
Change your mind,
And redefine your life.
Sometimes people want to see you fail
And it seems easier to follow suit.
But trust me when I say,
It is well worth the wait.
So fight,
To stay alive.
To thrive.
To enjoy your time
Without assholes
Dictating your next line.

I can go on living
Without the ghost of you.
As you are not dead,
There is no ghost to follow through.
I don't know where you are,
Who you are,
Or who you will be.
I do not care,
Or so I convince myself to believe.
When you dare to cross my mind,
I banish the thought,
And though
The humiliation I feel,
Shatters me from time to time
I have learned
That it is not an impossible task,
To take back what's mine.

Happiness is so elusive.
I fill myself with pills,
Utilize my coping skills,
Breathe,
Eat,
Sleep,
Repeat.
All to earn that special little chemical.

And yet . . . and yet,
Happiness is still a mystery to me.
I wanted it, I craved it,
I put in the work and earned it,
Yet some people get it for free.
They do not go through
Serotonin withdrawal,
They have an endless supply
Flying high, high, high.

I am envious of them.
For though I get the sweet release now,
I remember the dark pits of hell,
I once lived within,
Before this cherry friend squeezed its way in.
I still get flashbacks of the past,
While I grasp onto my future.
There is a part of me that thinks it's all a lie,
That I don't deserve
What I have rightfully earned.
Right now, the side of me that dares to
Hope,
Dream,
Fight,
And believe,

Is in the lead.
And I will do everything I can,
For that to continue to be,
Because I am a human
Who has struggled and grieved,
And I am no less deserving of happiness,
Than any other being.

I do not believe in revenge,
But I believe in karma.
And for you, I shall think,
The sweetest kiss of all,
Would be to fall off
The face of the Earth.
To be forgotten by all.
To be totally alone,
To achieve nothing notable.
With this kiss
It is done,
You can't take it back,
Karma will see to that.
Have fun in the abyss.
I promise,
You will not be missed.

Learning to trust
Has been a tumultuous task.
I am not used to
Sitting still,
Letting others do what they will,
With my story, my presence, and my friendship.
But I think one day,
I will.

I feel as if,
I have forgotten how to be human
Within this world
And this life I have been given.
I don't fit a mold.
I am not the model citizen normal people envision.
And to be in society as less than a dream,
Seems like an insurmountable feat.
At least to me.
But I remind myself there is always tomorrow,
There are infinite chances
To learn, to teach,
To grow and seek,
And to become the human
I am meant to be.

I am feminine,
I am pretty,
I am kind,
And none of these things are a crime.
None of these things justify,
The audacity of insecure guys.
I did not choose the shell I live in,
I cannot change
No matter how much I try
Or how much you want me to comply.
Why don't we instead teach our men,
That they can simply
Change their behavior,
Because
Women are not made for them.
We were made from fine wine,
Stars, and atoms.
Not to stand in a skirt,
Listen to your senseless words,
And lower ourselves for your self-worth.

I now have the capacity to say no,
Without feeling sorry for doing so.
I am confident in my appearance
And that it has nothing to do,
With outside interference.
I recognize my intelligence,
My strength,
My empathy and reliability.
I have a newfound confidence in myself.
In my ability to claim,
My story, my way.
No matter what anyone will say.

Never and *always* don't fit here anymore.

I will never get better.
I will always feel like shit.

Throw these words away,
We are reinventing them today.
For when you're healing
There is nothing you can't do.
I know it sounds corny to say,
But believe me, healing is no game.

Always and *never* were the devils on my shoulder,
Constraining and containing
The best parts of me
That I wasn't allowed to perceive.
Now that I am free,
I see,
That *Always* and *Never* can be
Such contradictory,
Meaningless things.
Wouldn't you agree?

I believe stubbornness and spite,
Have been given a negative connotation,
When it motivates me immensely.

Stubbornness,
Resilience,
Or perseverance.

Spite,
Bitterness,
Or resentment.

Whatever euphemism you choose,
Or critique you prefer
I'll define these words on my terms.

Stubbornness and spite
Are my sugar and spice.
And with them by my side,
I'll keep trudging and moving,
Speaking and growing up,
Proving those wrong,
Who have doubted me
For far too long.
I can make new choices.
My future is up to me,
My future *is* me.

Stubbornness and spite,
My ally,
My guide,
Will not let me down this time.

The simplest things can bring a tear to my eye,
A slight pressure on my heart,
And a peaceful air in my mind.

Sometimes seeing the sun and clouds
Or the night's shining stars,
Give me solace within my war-torn heart.
Other times it's
A glass of cold water,
The softness of my bed,
Or smiling with a friend,
That makes me believe
That this happiness won't end.

The fact that I can be content,
With the smallest of pleasures,
Of a mortal existence and end,
Makes me cry tears of
Joy,
Fulfillment,
And amends.
I will not take this feeling for granted again.

Loving myself,
Is not giving a fuck
About how society
Tells me to
Feel,
Heal,
Grow,
And forgive.

I'm going to do it my way,
By loving my body,
Eating when I want,
Reading through the day,
Sleeping till noon,
And breathing in deep too.

Supporting myself,
Learning to be alone,
Singing angry songs,
Screaming at the void.
Reveling in silence

Writing and using my voice.
For I have something up my sleeve,
A new perspective and a lesson
On how not to give a fuck.
It's simple but,
This is how I will fulfill my own needs.

You hugged me when I was scared.
You blocked me from prying eyes.
You believed me when I needed you.
You choose me time after time.
You helped me,
Supported me,
And loved me.
Through the anger,
The pain, the sadness, the rage.
Why? I will never know.
And though you're no longer there,
And the end of our days was unfair,
I know we both still care.
So, *thank you* from the bottom of my heart,
For choosing me instead of them.
Thank you for doing what most people don't.
I Love you,
And thank you for giving me hope.

When my mind tripped me,
You helped to pick me back up.
When my heart ached,
You provided a safe space.
When I am with you all
I feel at home,
I know I'm not alone.
Whether I'm speaking through tears,
Or laughing away my fears,
You listen to me,
Let me speak,
And comfort me in my time of need.
And I sincerely hope I can do the same
For all you lovely warriors.
I promise we will:
Heal hearts,
Heal minds,
And connect back to life.
I can never profess,
The amount of gratitude I possess
For each and every one of you.
I love you,
continue to fight,
Because I'll be there for you
At every step.

I have so many to thank
For keeping me safe,
While I was in
My most vulnerable place.

Mama, you lent me your strength,
Your heart was so large,
It was almost too much to take,
But I savor it to this day.

Dad, you made me smile
From ear to ear.
Giving your attention
And bear hugs,
You dried my tears
And calmed my fears.

Brother,
We have been through too much.
But it connects us together,
In silence or thunder.
Your loyalty and honesty
Are eternally there.

Grandma and Grandpa,
You taught me resilience.
If you can grow up
With the world betting against you,
Then I can too.
You taught me that my voice had meaning,
I'm so glad I listened to you.

And even though I'm a writer
My
Love,
Respect,
And Gratitude
For you,
Cannot be surmised with a simple rhyme.
Not even I,
Can give you a proper *Thank You.*

Forgiveness
Is such a powerful tool,
But do not be fooled,
I will not give it easily.
Not to Dumb and Dumber,
At least.
They don't deserve
To even grovel at my feet.
I have places to be and time to spend,
Forgiving myself, while I continue to mend.

I forgive myself,
I honestly do.
I was a naive child,
What was I to do?
But I know now,
The thing to do
Is cut the weeds out,
And plant new roots.

I know it is not my fault,
Nor should I rot in shame.
I deserve love,
I am worthy,
I have the right to live
And to forgive myself
For the turmoil I entertained.

Love is the key,
To all that is virtuous and bright.
But once that love is broken,
It's a fight for your life.
To love yourself once more,
Get back up on your feet,
And love the world around you,
Though often it is rather bleak.
Learn to appreciate the love you receive
And breathe it in deep.
Take a moment to get to know yourself.

I know that The Bodies still haunt me,
But they also taught me to seek, to speak.
The glass box can fracture,
And you can make something beautiful
With the debris.
The water will cleanse you.
Your mind will not forsake you,
And neither will your words.
They will catch up with your heart,
No longer needing time apart.
It all comes together eventually,
As hard as it may seem,
It can be done, just look at me.
I grew up to succeed
This is not the End,
It's a new Beginning.

Acknowledgments

THOUGH I HAVE THANKED plenty of people within my book, many more deserve recognition for helping It Starts with the End come to fruition. Firstly, to my publishers as Wipf & Stock, thank you for taking a chance on me. I know the subject of my book is not the most marketable or easy to read, but you allowed me to share my story unincumbered. For that, I am forever grateful. To my immediate family, your enthusiasm and support were instrumental in me even finishing this book. To all my friends who proofread over and over again, thank you for calming my anxious brain and giving me clarity. Lastly, to all the courageous survivors, I hope I did justice to our shared experiences and that you found some strength or hope throughout reading. Thank You all.

CPSIA information can be obtained
at www.ICGtesting.com
Printed in the USA
LVHW080601261022
731606LV00021B/361

9 781666 751970